First World War
and Army of Occupation
War Diary
France, Belgium and Germany

23 DIVISION
69 Infantry Brigade,
Brigade Trench Mortar Battery
1 July 1916 - 31 October 1917

WO95/2184/6

The Naval & Military Press Ltd
www.nmarchive.com
Published in association with The National Archives

Published by

The Naval & Military Press Ltd

Unit 10 Ridgewood Industrial Park,

Uckfield, East Sussex,

TN22 5QE England

Tel: +44 (0) 1825 749494

www.naval-military-press.com

www.nmarchive.com

This diary has been reprinted in facsimile from the original. Any imperfections are inevitably reproduced and the quality may fall short of modern type and cartographic standards.

© **Crown Copyright**
Images reproduced by permission of The National Archives, London, England, 2015.

Contents

Document type	Place/Title	Date From	Date To
Heading	WO95/2184/6 23 Div Brigade Trench Mortar Battery Aug, Sep Oct 1916 Jan, Feb, Mar, Apr, May + Aug 1917 Missing.		
Heading	23rd Division 69th Infy Bde 69th Lt Trench Mortar Bty Jly 1916-1917 Oct.		
War Diary		01/07/1916	31/07/1916
Heading	23 Division 69 Infantry Brigade Brigade Trench Mortar Battery. Aug, Sept & Oct 1916 Missing.		
War Diary		01/11/1916	31/12/1916
Heading	23 Division 69 Infantry Brigade Brigade Trench Mortar Battery Jan To May 1917 Missing		
War Diary	In The Field	01/06/1917	31/07/1917
Heading	23 Division 69 Infantry Brigade Brigade Trench Mortar Battery Aug 1917 Missing.		
War Diary	In The Field	01/09/1917	29/09/1917
Miscellaneous	Appendix "A" Report On Operation 19/9/16-20/9/16	19/09/1916	19/09/1916
Miscellaneous	Group D. 3 Gun At1 I 15 d 33. Zillebeke Bund (c H.Q).	29/10/1916	29/10/1916
War Diary	Field	01/10/1917	31/10/1917
Heading	10th W. Riding 23 Vol. 7		
Heading	9th Yorkshires 23 Vol 7		
Heading	8th Yorkshires 23 Vol		
Heading	11th West Yorks 23rd Div Vol 1		
Heading	8 Lab Reg Vol 8 23		
Heading	69 M G Coy Vol 2 23		

WO 95 2184/6

23 DN

Brigade Trench Mortar
Battery

AUG, SEP, OCT 1916
JAN, FEB, MAR, APR, MAY + AUG 1917 } missing

1917 OCT

WAR DIARY

INTELLIGENCE SUMMARY

Army Form C. 2118

July

23 / Vol 1

69th Light Trench Mortar Battery

74 %
Dec '17

Place	Date	Hour	Summary of Events and Information
	July 1st		Marched from COISY to BAIZIEUX
	2nd		Moved to bivouacs about ¾ mile N.W of ALBERT.
	3rd	12. noon	Moved to bivouacs beside ALBERT — BECOURT WOOD road.
		7.30 p.m	Four guns & half personnel moved into trenches at SCOTS REDOUBT, in support of 6/11th West Yorks. to positions no ammunition were taken over, as no information could be obtained as to the whereabouts of the T.M.D of the Brigade relieved.
	4th		Remaining four guns taken into front line supporting 9th Yorks.
	5th		About fifty rounds fired to assist 11th N. Yorks. Bomb attack. Four guns were advanced up and to fire across to the right, where the 10th West Ridings were held up, but owing to enemy counter attack these guns had to retire to old positions. Later enemy endeavoured to bomb down trench own line, but desisted on our firing thirty rounds.
		5. p.m	During advance of 9th Yorks continuous fire was kept up on enemy machine guns until our men got too close for further firing. This machine gun did not fire during the advance of the men, was found in a dugout.
		8. p.m	One gun was advanced to new front trench, but was sent back.
	6th		Relieved by 68th T.M.D. Moved to bivouacs near BELLEVUE FARM.

Army Form C. 2118.

WAR DIARY
or
INTELLIGENCE SUMMARY.

by 7th Light Trench Mortar Battery

(Erase heading not required.)

Place	Date	Hour	Summary of Events and Information	Remarks and references to Appendices
	July 7th		In Div. reserve at BELLEVUE FARM. Moved to bivouacs at BECOURT WOOD.	
	8th		Moved to billets in ALBERT	
	9th		Stood fast	
	10th		Moved into position for attack on CONTALMAISON, left half battery in trench N of BAILIFF WOOD, guarding left flank of 11th W. Yorks. Enemy made no attempt on this flank only a few rounds were fired to register. Right half battery supported 8th Yorks from trench S. of CONTALMAISON. Fired about 50 rounds at machine gun positions in village.	
	11th		Relieved by 1st T.M.B.	
	12th		Marched to FRANVILLERS	
	13th		Moved to MOLLIENS AU BOIS	
	14th - 20th		Stood fast	
	21st		Marched to MILLENCOURT	
	22nd - 25th		Stood fast	
	26th		Took over billets in ALBERT from 2nd Brigade.	
	27th		Officer carried out reconnaissance	
	28th		Relieved 68th T.M.B. Fired in support of bomb attack on MUNSTER ALLEY	

Army Form C. 2118.

WAR DIARY
or
~~INTELLIGENCE SUMMARY.~~
(Erase heading not required.)

Place	Date	Hour	Summary of Events and Information	Remarks and references to Appendices
	July 29th		In action at MUNSTER ALLEY. Fired at intervals during the day on SWITCH line from GLOSTER ALLEY.	
	30th		do.	
	31st		About 100 rounds fired on MUNSTER ALLEY.	

G. L. Lehman Capt.
Ot. 69th Light Trench Mortar Battery.

23 Division
69 Infantry Brigade
Brigade Trench Mortar Battery.
Aug, Sept & Oct 1916 missing

Army Form C. 2118.

WAR DIARY
or
INTELLIGENCE SUMMARY.
(Erase heading not required.)

69th Trench Mortar Battery   Vol 5

Place	Date	Hour	Summary of Events and Information	Remarks and references to Appendices
In Left Sector	Nov. 1.		2 Offensive positions. 3 Defensive.	
	2-8		No firing	
	9		Relieved by 70th T.M.B. & moved to EERIE Camp.	
	10		Took over Right Sector from 68th T.M.B. 4 guns in the line. Relief completed 3.50 pm	
	11		10 Rounds fired in retaliation to enemy Trench Mortars.	
	12		40 Rounds fired in retaliation	
	13		20 " " "	
	14		no firing	
	15		32 rounds fired into suspected M.G. Emplacement.	
	16		27 rounds fired from No. 4 Gun at 6.0 pm Gun situated L.24.D.87.23. Patrol reports good results	
	17		nil	
	19		33 rounds fired. 8 for registration purposes.	
	20		75 rounds fired in support of raid.	
	21		nil	
	22		Relieved by 70th T.M.B. moved to EERIE Camp.	
	29		Relieved 68th T.M.B. in Left Sector. Relief completed 3.0 PM	
	30		no firing	

4-12-16.

E. J. Buchanan Capt.
O.C. 69th T.M.B.

Army Form C. 2118.

WAR DIARY
or
INTELLIGENCE SUMMARY.
(Erase heading not required.)

69th T.M Battery
M Company

Place	Date	Hour	Summary of Events and Information	Remarks and references to Appendices
	1916.			
	Dec 1.		In Left Sector. Round fired for registration purposes.	
	2.		80 rounds fired from Vigo Street upon enemy front line.	
	3 & 4		No firing	
	5.		6 rounds fired in retaliation to enemy Rifle Grenades which ceased in retaliation.	
	6.		7 " " " " " "	
	7.		15 " " " " " "	
	7–14		No firing	
	15.		Relieved by 70th T.M.B. moved to EERIE CAMP.	
	23.		Relieved 68th T.M.B. in Right Sector. Relief completed 3.30 p.m.	
	24–26		No firing	
	27.		17½ rounds fired on to enemy front & support lines in retaliation to enemy Trench Mortars.	
	28 & 29		No firing	
	30.		22 rounds fired on to enemy front line, with good results.	
	31.		100 rounds fired on to enemy front & support lines in retaliation to enemy Trench Mortars.	

4-1-17.

W. J. Munn 2nd Lt
for O.C. 69th T.M. Battery

23 DIVISION
69 INFANTRY BRIGADE
BRIGADE TRENCH MORTAR BATTERY.
JAN TO MAY 1917 MISSING

Army Form C. 2118.

59th L.T.M.B. June 1917.

WAR DIARY
or
INTELLIGENCE SUMMARY.
(Erase heading not required.)

Place	Date	Hour	Summary of Events and Information	Remarks and references to Appendices
In the field	June 2nd		Moved from Billets in STEENVOORDE area to Camp at L.3.5.6.2.5. (Sheet 2B)	
	June 3rd		Having carried out above camp moved from camp at L.3.5.6.2.5. to "L" Camp near BUSSE BOOM.	
	June 4th		Stayed at above camp.	
	June 5th		Moved from "L" Camp to South COPSE where we bivouaced until the night of the 6th June. We then moved into position preparatory to attack which took place on the following day.	
	June 7th		Attack took place at 3.10 a.m. during which we suffered casualties of 2 Officers killed. 2 O.R.'s killed 1 Officer Wounded. 12 O.R.'s wounded. There was very little firing required from us on this date, only about 100 rounds being fired during the whole operations. 2 N.C.O's and 4 men did exceptionally good work and have since been awarded the Military Medal.	
	June 8th		No firing was done by us on this date, as several working parties were engaged in carrying ammn to the guns. Casualties on this date 2 O.R.'s wounded.	
	June 9th		16 rounds were fired & prompt reply to our S.O.S signal which was sent. Tump. but we lost one life. We suffered no casualties. Ammunition carrying continued.	

WAR DIARY or INTELLIGENCE SUMMARY

Place	Date	Hour	Summary of Events and Information	Remarks and references to Appendices
In the field	June 10th		No firing done by us to-day. Casualties 3 O.R's wounded. Carrying parties employed on carrying ammn. to guns.	
	June 11th		We fired 20 rounds on to enemy's patrol opposite IMPARTIAL AV. enemy retired immediately. We opened fire. Casualties 10 O.R wounded.	
	June 12th		No firing done as this flak hut each gun was made up with 100 rounds leaving about 90 rounds with each one. Relieved by 19th C.T.M.B. about midnight after which we were marched to VANCOUVER CAMP.	
	June 13th		During the day the men were allowed to rest until evening when we moved from VANCOUVER CAMP to the BERTHEN AREA.	
	June 14th		The day was spent in cleaning guns, carts etc. Kit inspection in the afternoon.	
	June 15th		Shaving carried out.	
	June 16th		Inspection of Bttn. by G.O.C. Division. During the afternoon special instruction in map reading was given to the Battery.	

WAR DIARY
or
INTELLIGENCE SUMMARY.

(Erase heading not required.)

Army Form C. 2118.

Place	Date	Hour	Summary of Events and Information	Remarks and references to Appendices
In the field	June 1st / June 28th		Training carried out. Special attention being paid to Instruction in Tactical handling Stoke's Mortars in Semi open warfare, map reading, and instruction in use of compass.	
	June 29th		During this period 16 new men joined the battery and received special instruction on the gun.	
	June 30th		Moved from Training Area to Camp near RENINGHELST. Moved into line and relieved 72nd L.T.M.B. the firing was close on this date and we suffered no casualties.	

A. Markham. Captain
O.C. 69th Light Trench Mortar Battery

69th L.T.M.B.

Army Form C. 2118.

WAR DIARY
or
INTELLIGENCE SUMMARY.
(Erase heading not required.)

July 1917

Place	Date	Hour	Summary of Events and Information	Remarks and references to Appendices
	July 1st		In the line.	
	2		Another gun put in line to cover point near KLEIN ZILLEBEKE.	
	3		Relieved by 141st T.M.B. Moved to Mic Mac Camp.	
	4		Entrained at OUDERDOM Sidings 3-30 p.m. Detrained GODEWAERSVELDE	
	5		Marched from there to billets in STEENWOORDE area (about J.33.B. sheet 27)	
			Training	
	6		do	
	7		Moved into STEENWOORDE	
	8		Training	
	9		do.	
	10		do.	
	11		do.	
	12		Entrained GODEWAERSVELDE. Detrained OUDERDOM Sidings. Marched to Mic Mac camp.	
	13		Relieved 68th T.M.B. OBERS RIDGE Section. 6 guns in line. Relief completed 11-30 p.m.	
	14		No firing	
	15		do.	

Army Form C. 2118.

WAR DIARY
or
INTELLIGENCE SUMMARY.
(Erase heading not required.)

Instructions regarding War Diaries and Intelligence Summaries are contained in F. S. Regs., Part II. and the Staff Manual respectively. Title pages will be prepared in manuscript.

Place	Date	Hour	Summary of Events and Information	Remarks and references to Appendices
	July 1917			
	16th		No firing.	
	17th		3 rounds fired from gun situated in ILLUSIVE SUPPORT for registration purposes.	
	18th		2 rounds fired from gun situated I.30.b.35.72. 2 rounds fired from gun situated I.30.b.40.05. for registration purposes. 33 rounds in all fired from guns situated I.36.b.25 and I.30.b.40.05. during enemy's bombardment of our lines on night of 16/17.	
	19th		A direct hit was obtained by the enemy during night on an ammunition dump of the mortar in ILLUSIVE SUPPORT. The gun and 200 rounds were blown up.	
	20th		Gun near HEDGE St. blown up about 11-30 p.m. Ammunition intact.	
	21st		No firing.	
	22nd		Relieved by 72nd T.M.B.	
	23rd		Marched to Mt. des CATS arrived in billets 6-20 p.m. 26.d. 5.D.	
	24th		Training	
	25th		"	
	26th		Marched to and entrained at CAESTRE. Detrained St. OMER. Marched to BEISINGHEM	

Army Form C. 2118.

WAR DIARY
or
INTELLIGENCE SUMMARY.
(Erase heading not required.)

Instructions regarding War Diaries and Intelligence Summaries are contained in F.S. Regs., Part II. and the Staff Manual respectively. Title pages will be prepared in manuscript.

Place	Date	Hour	Summary of Events and Information	Remarks and references to Appendices
	July 1917			
	27th		Training.	
	28th		do	
	29th		Rifle Range	
	30th		Training	
	31st		do.	

Adamson. Captain.
O.C. 69th L.T.M.B.

23 DIVISION
69 INFANTRY BRIGADE
BRIGADE TRENCH MORTAR BATTERY
AUG 1917 MISSING.

694 L.T.M.B

Army Form C. 2118.

WAR DIARY
or
INTELLIGENCE SUMMARY.
(Erase heading not required.)

September 1917

Place	Date	Hour	Summary of Events and Information	Remarks and references to Appendices
In the field	Sept 1st 1917		In huts near DICKEBUSCH	Map References Belgium Sheet 28
	2		Marched to STEENVOORDE	
	3		Marched from STEENVOORDE to LEDERZEELE	
	4/11		Training	
	12		Brigade Rehearsal	
	13		Marched to STEENVOORDE Area	
	14		Marched to ONTARIO CAMP (NR RENNINGHELST)	
	16		Moved to MIC MAC CAMP (DICKEBUSCH Area)	
	19/20		Moved up the line & stayed for dinner at RAILWAY DUGOUTS. Took over assembly positions in left Bde Sector behind INVERNESS COPSE. 3 Guns were detailed to advance from left of Bn Front & 2 from Right. All guns were to move forward following 1st Batt of Infantry. Two guns proceeded towards the TANK TRAP J.14.d.8.2. but got just before reaching it, a stray shell destroyed the guns & put the teams out of action. The remaining gun moved up left of COPSE and fired on S.P. at J.14.d.85.50. A hit on the doorway of Dug out was observed & the garrison surrendered. This gun then followed the W Riding Regt to the final Objective & took up position covering the valley of the REUTERBECK	

WAR DIARY
INTELLIGENCE SUMMARY.
(Erase heading not required.)

Army Form C. 2118.

Place	Date	Hour	Summary of Events and Information	Remarks and references to Appendices
	Sept 1917 19/20 (Cont)		Two guns on right moved forward behind Infantry to HERENTHAGE CHATEAU. They fired 3 rounds on S.P. about J.20.6. central (on the Right 13th Bdes) Object hit was observed. Shortly afterwards 30 Germans surrendered. The guns then followed the West Riding Regt forward & established themselves covering Centre & Right of Bde Front. At the guns position a light Meunenwerfer was found mounted. This was put out of action & a wood in which the enemy appeared to be massing was fired on continually during the afternoon abt 200 rounds being fired. At dusk the S.O.S. was sent up from front line and the 3 Stokes Mortars in position fired 160 rounds on S.O.S. line. About 50 rounds were also fired by the Meunenwerfer. Casualties 1.Off. 32 O.R. 3 Guns remaining in action. 5 Rounds fired at dusk in reply to S.O.S. Guns then buried & out of action till late in evening.	
	21		Guns withdrawn from line	
	22		Makers ammunition dumps in front of INVERNESS COPSE.	
	23		Relieved by 98th L.T.M.B. moved to Mic Mac Camp. After dinner moved to	
	24		ALBERTA CAMP (RENNINGHELST)	

Army Form C. 2118.

WAR DIARY
or
INTELLIGENCE SUMMARY.
(Erase heading not required.)

Instructions regarding War Diaries and Intelligence Summaries are contained in F. S. Regs., Part II. and the Staff Manual respectively. Title pages will be prepared in manuscript.

Place	Date	Hour	Summary of Events and Information	Remarks and references to Appendices
	Sept 1917			
	25		At Alberta Camp.	
	26		do	
	27		Moved by bus to DICKEBUSCH. After status relieved 98th & 7th/15 Near CLAPHAM JUNCTION	
	28		Men employed making forward ammunition dumps.	
	29		Two guns taken to CAMERON COVERT, covering left flank of Brigade	

Gordon Wright Lt
O.C. 69th T.M.B.

APPENDIX "A" page 1.

Report on Operation 19/9/16 - 20/9/16.
Sept 19th 1916

About 2.30 p.m. the enemy made a surprise attack on PRUE and STARFISH trenches held by "B" Coy 9th YORKS supported by one Vickers gun under L/Cpl Lewis. As the attack was made in considerable strength by bomb up 3 converging trenches and it was impossible to utilize M.G. fire, The O.C. trench 9th YORKS ordered L/Cpl Lewis to retire as quickly as possible with his guns. This he did, but owing to the speed of the attack was forced to abandon his tripod and ammunition. Casualties were 2 wounded and one missing. The 9th YORKS fell back to the SUNKEN ROAD with bombing stops in PRUE & STARFISH, one Vickers gun covering the open ground in the vicinity. Considerable fighting took place during the afternoon and night with the result that PRUE and STARFISH trenches were recovered up to about 100 yards page 2

of the original position.

The two guns of 2/Lieut LINDSAY in reserve took post in their battle positions in 70th Avenue, two guns of the Motor Machine Guns taking over the indirect fire which was being carried out.

Two guns of No 1 Section were sent up to cover ground to their right front on the ridge E of MARTINPUICH. These guns for the night were under the command of Lieut GRAYES.

APPENDIX "A" (Continued) page 3

Sept 20th 1916

The situation being reported again quiet Lieut GRAVES was ordered to rejoin HQs leaving his guns under Sgt. Cowling, these Guns coming under the direction of 2/Lieut SYMES and the 2 guns under 2/Lieut LINDSAY were ordered to rejoin HQs their place to be taken in case of attack by the 2 M.M.G. guns already mentioned. Special mention must be made of the excellent work done by the runners who succeeded in keeping communication open between the front line and headquarters under particularly arduous circumstances the heavy bombardment, the darkness of the night and the condition of the ground all rendering their work of great difficulty.

No 2 gun was at 11.30 am hit by a 4.2 shell and very badly damaged. Its place was immediately taken by the reserve gun from Advanced HQs and a gun from HQs sent up as reserve gun to advanced HQs. There were no casualties.

Sept 21st 1916.

The situation remained quiet and unchanged. In view of an intended raid on the enemy line M 26 C 2565 to M 26 b.73 the gun of 2/Lieut MARSH was pushed forward to a recently dug trench about M.26 b.24 and the page 4

Persh alley No 4 Gun to about M 26 d 5.4
The raid took place at 1 am. and the parties
returned by 2 am. having found the enemy trench
evacuated.

W.J.C. Robertson
OC 61 MGC

Group D.   3 guns at I 15 d 33. ZILLEBEKE
                    BUND. (a HQs)
In the event of attack these guns are now
under orders of OC Company.
Their normal positions will be
    (1) I 15 d 33. ZILLEBEKE BUND.
    (2) I 21 d 9.8 approx NORTH SHORE
    (3) I 16 c 75.75. MOATED GRANGE
From these positions they will cover ground in
SQUARE I 16 d & I 22 a &b.

GROUP E   4 guns at A.B.C L'ESTAMINET
YPRES. I 8 c 4.7.
In the event of attack two of these guns move up
to I 15 d 33. to replace guns moved from there.
Remaining two will move to ~~next post~~ RAMPARTS
I 14 b 14 & will be held there in reserve ready
for action

                    J G Roberts Capt
                    OC Coy MGC

Note to above 29/10/16
Ruined House gun moved to I 17 b 70.25 front
line
                    R&H

69th L.T.M.B.

Army Form C. 2118.

WAR DIARY
~~INTELLIGENCE~~ SUMMARY

October 1917.

(Erase heading not required.)

Instructions regarding War Diaries and Intelligence Summaries are contained in F.S. Regs., Part II. and the Staff Manual respectively. Title pages will be prepared in manuscript.

Place	Date	Hour	Summary of Events and Information	Remarks and references to Appendices
Field	October 1		In Line. Inverness Copse Sector. Two guns in CAMERON COVERT destroyed early in the morning by shell fire. ~~Retreat by~~ Moved to RIDGE WOOD CAMP about 9.0 pm.	
	2		Moved by bus to METEREN area.	
	3/9		Training	
	10		Moved to ONTARIO CAMP. [NEAR RENNINGHELST]	
	12		Moved to ANZAC CAMP.	
	13/22		At ANZAC CAMP. Men employed on carrying up the line etc.	
	23		Marched to VLAMERTINGHE, entrained. Detrained at WIZERNES. Marched to BARLINGHEM.	
	24		Training	
	25/28		do	
	29		Inspected by G.O.C. Division	
	30		Training	
	31		Inspected by the Commander-in-Chief.	

[signature] Lt.
Comdg. 69th Light T.M. Battery

10th W. Riding
tob: 7

23

6. Y.
17 mile

23 9th Yorkshires
       Vol 7

                                J.A.
                              g.shuts

8th Yorkshires
23   Vol: 5

11th West
Yorks
23rd Div

Vol. 1

8 Jak Reg
vol 6
238

69 McCoy
Vol 2

23